About the Trainer

Marilyn first entered the dog-training world in 1968, is a Member of the British Institute of Professional Dog Trainers and has professionally taught dogs and owners for over 30 years. In 1972 she founded the Shepperton Dog Training Club. The demand was such that she found herself training as many as 200 dogs a week. At the last count, more than 19,000 dogs have benefited from her tuition. Marilyn initially designed and introduced the 'SoundPlay' method, for dogs with problem behaviour – which proved so successful that it's now been incorporated into all her training programmes. Back in the '80's you may remember seeing Marilyn and some of her younger students on television's 'Freetime'. She also appeared in one of Japan's canine documentaries. Marilyn's approach is most definitely non-confrontational. Observing Natural Canine Behaviour has played a large part in Marilyn's approach. She encourages owners to appreciate the nature of the dog – in order to successfully teach a dog, we first need to understand him.

Also available:

Books:
More Essentials for the Domestic Dog Owner plus Classroom
(lessons 7 – 12)

Videos:
Essentials for the Domestic Dog Owner plus Classroom
(lessons 1 – 6)

More Essentials for the Domestic Dog Owner plus Classroom
(lessons 7 – 12)

All 'Essential' Books and Videos can be obtained from:
books@soundplaydogs.com, Amazon Books, High Street Stationers or
direct from our distributors, M.R.Printers:

MR Printers
43 Marloborough Road
Yeovil
Somerset
BA21 5JW

Acknowledgements

One of my greatest satisfactions in life is having had the opportunity to work with dogs and their owners for most of it. 'Essentials for the Domestic Dog Owner' contains some of the answers to questions and problems most commonly addressed over the last 33 years. I would like to thank each and every dog owner that I've met and spoken to – without your questions, I'd have not been stimulated to write this book. I would also like to thank those who have helped make this book possible: my SoundPlay colleagues, Jason Walmsley, Donna Carl, Louise Blackman and Janet Ulliott; Shirley, Marion, Becky, Sharon and Bob, all of whom have suffered my hard-fast rules while studying and assisting. Also Jerry and Jason from America – whom I've spent many an hour on-line, debating most aspects of canine behaviour and training. Of course I'd like to thank my dogs (here and gone) – Princess, Duke, Merlin, Jenny, Bonnie, Misty, Petra, Whisky, Polar and Sheba for trusting, teaching and understanding me; Alan Brock without whom this book would be far from editorially correct; Geoff Williams for Photography, Layout and Design. Most of all, I'd like to thank my family and friends – particularly my daughters, Julie and Malina, who've always been supportive and understanding when my time's been restricted. Their high standards, unselfishness attitude, loyalty, love and devotion is a true example of how a non-confrontational upbringing is always the best.

Contents

To Julie and Malina - also, Petra

X X X

Petra 1990

My First Dog

As far back as my very first memory, my dream as a child was to have a dog of my own. We'd had family dogs of course, but I yearned that special bond only seen in Lassie films. At last, when 16 my wish came true - my very own German Shepherd, 'Princess'. We didn't have a lot of money, and Dad made the mistake of buying the cheapest German Shepherd he could find. Unbeknown to us at the time, she was interbred by travellers. She was a nightmare!!! She attacked everyone she saw, wouldn't come back, pulled on the lead, howled, barked and whined constantly. I took her training and she failed the course FOUR times. Instructors at the school told me she couldn't be trained and she'd have to be put down!!! **Everyone** told me she'd have to be put down!!! Except ONE man - Eric Irvine, my first real tutor, a man I'll never forget. I remember the moment I'd just been told by one of the instructors: 'Your dog can't be trained'. I burst into tears, then said 'NO! She can! If you won't help me, I'll go somewhere else'. Eric overheard, and said 'You think you can do it'? I said 'I WILL do it'. He paused a moment, then said 'Meet me in the park Sunday Morning 10 am sharp'. A year later she was as perfect as a dog can be. That's why I never give up on a dog, and unless there's a medical reason, refuse to believe there's a dog that cannot be taught to behave well, within a domestic environment. Eric taught me many things, but the most vital lesson of all was awareness. To 'feel' the way a dog thinks – become a unit, working with, not against. Together – a team. I'm not sure if everyone can learn this – for some it's natural. After reading this book, you'll **know** if you're a natural!!!

Polar pup

Sheba 2 weeks old

Whisky 2000

Why do some Dogs always come back ?

Some Traditional Training dictates that we have to 'check' a dog towards us and command 'COME' to teach the Recall. We have to show our dog who's the boss!!! If that doesn't work we use a long lead - let him run off and yell 'COME' as his neck reaches the end.   **Painful !!!** Should 'Come' mean pain? Surely our dog wouldn't trust us. Besides, if we want our dog to come back to us, shouldn't we aim to be more attractive than anything else, not less? (See Polar's enthusiasm during Recall Conditioning)

Question: What would painful training condition our dog to associate with the word 'Come'?

A sound that interrupts fun and causes pain

Question: Doesn't sound right - what can we do instead?

Condition our dog to become excited and attracted to us, immediately we say 'Come'.

Question: Makes more sense...How can we do that?

First, we make a list of all the things our dog is attracted to. The sound of our keys — usually means we're going out. Rough and tumble play, chasing, fetching, chewing, tugging. Being praised and **Attention!** We can make use of all these attractions and link them together, associating them to the word 'COME'. We need to **'condition'** our dog to a sound, whereby the response will be to come to us. We could of course consider food as an attraction, but we can't be sure to have this with us everywhere we go; also, some dogs aren't turned on that much by treats and some easily gain weight.

The Recall Conditioning Exercise

This exercise served two purposes: Firstly it should, if our timing's right, give a 100% recall no matter what the distractions, and secondly it's great for losing those unwanted lbs.! Try it.

While in the park (on long lead), call your dog when s/he's **not** engaged in something else. Do this **without** allowing the lead to become tight. **Say 'Come'/Chink keys (ONCE) – immediately praise, and keep praising as you run the other way excitedly.** When dog catches up, play rough, exciting and invigorating games for a few moments before sending off again (- tug of war, chase me, fetch at short distances – use silly and exhilarating voice sounds to stimulate more interest). Use every bit of verbal and physical energy you have to attract the dog to you. (if the other people in the park don't think you're insane, you need to be more exuberant). One last praise and give a signal to go off again – **('Go-on then, off you go').** Relax and stroll a little. Repeat again and again until you're both exhausted. Every once in a while, just chink and call your dog in and release again without play. Other times, chink and call your dog in, walk towards the car (or even into the car) and then back out to the park again. When you're confident and only when in safe area, chink and call dog in, unhook lead, send out again and do all above without lead. Always run away from dog when calling in...... and play hide and seek every now and then (note: some dogs are intimidated by rough play - In these cases just play 'chase me').

What is this doing?

It's Pavlovian Conditioning – You're conditioning the dog to respond to a chosen stimulus (sound of the keys and the word 'come') occurring just before the conditioned response – eager arousal, associated with you. The dog will be conditioned to come to you. Also, by letting him go off again, you're not trapping him by calling him to you. He won't associate coming to you as being 'end of fun' or 'time to go home'. Soon, you'll be able to socialise him without fears. He plays with other dogs for a while. You call – he comes – you release. He finds something disgusting to sniff. You call – he comes – you release. Remember to always give the release command **('Go-on then, off you go').** This will keep him seeing you as the source of freedom - to all those positive feelings he'll experience while running and playing. Remember initially only to call your dog when he's not engaged in some other high drive activity. Until you've shown him how thrilling it is to "come" when called, you won't be able to compete with a playful group of dogs, or the scent of something to hunt. Also remember, when its time to go - put lead on, and keep it exciting. Run to the car, then back to the park. Release him again **('Go-on then off you go').** Call him. Lead on again. Run to the car. Running is exciting and fun......... and it keeps us healthy!

What is SoundPlay?

SoundPlay is a positive, no force, no punishment, non-confrontational dog teaching method, addressing long-term canine domestication and behaviour modification. No punishment (physical or verbal) – no intimidation – no food rewards. SoundPlay works to put into perspective the differences between human and dog communication.

Issues such as intentions and/or responses to thoughts and emotions are considered and explored. For instance, if our dog shows what we see as aggression, and we respond in an equally aggressive manner, what message are we communicating? To our dog, we're demonstrating the same emotion, aggression, hence confirming our approval of its actions- we are joining in the game. If while teaching heel and recall, we become unfair and use negative reinforcement, (yelling, tight lead, collar check, hitting etc.), our dog will not understand, become anxious and lose trust in our judgement –responding out of fear, not respect.

Fear, and suppressed emotions/desires, can lead to phobias. Dogs must be motivated, not punished. If we reprimand a particular type of behaviour, (e.g.: barking, chewing, digging, nipping) it doesn't make sense to the dog – we stifle an emotion or desire and while closing the door on that particular behaviour, we may, in so doing, open the door to alternative behaviours, which might be far worse.

By failing to recognise our dog's nature, we're showing incompetence. SoundPlay recognises the importance of canine natural drives and designs games to stimulate, motivate, and satisfy, combined with the use of sound conditioning in training our dog. Sound Conditioning is essential to our program.

Sound distraction is scientifically proven to be highly effective. We interrupt a behaviour, introduce an alternative, alter a mood or attract, without making an issue of that behaviour. We emphasise that dogs don't recognise any behaviour as *wrong*. If we look at all the behaviours we need to inter-rupt we will realise that they are all vital to the survival of the canine spe-cies in the wild - chewing, barking, digging, scenting, chasing, biting, breed-ing, etc.

Some Traditional training vs. SoundPlay:
Some Traditional training - Dog pulling on lead: some Traditional training depends on jerking lead and commanding 'heel', where the command 'heel' is given *at the same time* the dog is pulling – therefore the dog will identify the 'pulling' with the sound 'heel'. The dog thereafter believes s/he is obey-ing the command 'heel' by keeping the lead tight. Also, tension on the col-lar/lead will cause the dog to pull harder (a natural response).
Question: What would this method have the dog associate with the com-mand 'heel'?
Answer: *Confusion, Anxiety, and the command 'heel' always accompanies a sore neck!* Additionally, there is no reward for it's efforts to pull, so anxiety develops. Eventually, through trial and error, the dog finds an alternative position that is less painful, and/or accepts that walking with his owner 'is' painful and he has no choice but to grin and bear it. Alas though – the dog has doubts about his owner's trustworthiness!
SoundPlayDogs Method – To TEACH, we use verbal and body signals to identify the dog's action *'but only while he's doing the action'*, as opposed to when he's not *!* We **never** reprimand. We create situations where the dog has no alternative but to choose (and desire) to respond in the way we direct. Good Dog Training is 'Identifying & Organising Behaviour', rather than 'Stopping Behaviour'.
Reward V's Punishment: SoundPlay recognises that reward increases posi-tive motivation. SoundPlay has therefore designed a training program that focuses on positive and stimulating teaching methods. SoundPlay eliminates punishment completely and absolutely abandons the force/fear/intimidation training theories where all true motivation is stifled.
Conditioning to Sound & Sound Tool: The level of success is dependent on the efficiency, accuracy, know-how, **and awareness** of the handler. The sound used is a single chink o**f an ordinary set of keys or the 'SoundPlay Chinx'**. To effectively *condition our dog to sound* we use several excellent sound-con-ditioning exercises. We must develop precision timing, co-ordination, voice control and body language. It's *essential* that instant prolonged praise *im-mediately* follows the voice, body and sound signal. Unlike most traditional methods, we don't run to a standard sequential program – Heel, Sit, Down,

Stay, Come, Hold, Give, etc. SoundPlay has the advantage of being able to deal with whatever may be important at any given time. Generally our first consideration is trust.

I think the easiest way to put the whole idea into perspective is to always remember that we can be verbally firm whenever we're instructing a dog 'what he should do' (once he's learned how to do it). However, we never engage in trying to instruct him 'what he must not do'. I personally refuse to believe they understand what isn't there.

Therefore, we distract them from the behaviour we don't want, then immediately create a situation where they employ an alternative behaviour we do want, which we immediately reward with praise. The new behaviour then becomes far more worthwhile to our dog. Once 'conditioned' we can nearly always use 'come' as a default when interrupting a behaviour – therefore once learned (and as 'come' is a doing word), we can be as firm with the instruction as is necessary at that particular time.

SoundPlay Sound Distraction

Interrupting and Stopping a behaviour: (Barking, howling, Chewing, Nipping, Digging, Growling etc.) Understanding Sound Distraction may be easy, but believing in it comes only when we see the amazing results. Results depend on self-discipline, consistency, confident accurate handling, precise timing, good verbal ability and a new-found awareness. Once a handler has worked to achieve these abilities, the technique **will** work. Sound Distraction is extremely effective in modifying behaviours, (long term, and without creating an alternative, far worse behaviour such as aggression, self mutilation and mounting). Its effectiveness is such that when conditioning is properly addressed, recall will also be completely reliable. Those who try the technique, and find their dog becomes nervous, are with respect, doing it wrongly. Sound Conditioning increases confidence if applied correctly. In my opinion, one reason a dog shows anxiety is because he feels vulnerable – does not trust his owner to be able to cope efficiently with a situation and reacts adversely. If we identify this and act accordingly (interrupt anxious thoughts and replace with positive thoughts) we are reversing his assessment of the situation. However, if we play the barking game along side him (yell and reprimand), we are increasing his anxiety and showing that we too are anxious. We have seen, by observing and studying a significant number of video stills, that sound will immediately interrupt thought processes and behaviour, (barking for instance), yet the response shown is sometimes too minuscule for us to detect at normal speed. Here is why we must praise immediately after the point of sound interruption (we are praising for that unseen response). Although we suggest keys or the SoundPlay Chinx Tool, any sudden sound will interrupt thought, and as long as it is followed by immediate prolonged non-physical praise, this will give the dog a new perspective on the situation. Sound is not a miracle cure however, and cannot be assumed to work wonders without a scientific understanding of what we're actually doing. **(Sound Conditioning exercises are essential – see SoundPlay Classroom)** One sound interruption, although effective subconsciously, is not necessarily going to result in permanent stoppage of that behaviour. Several interruptions may be necessary. In-fact it's essential that we continue to interrupt until the behaviour stops completely on that occasion. Think of it as a battle of wills – us competing with our dog – who's going to have the last word. It doesn't have to be a boxing match though, it can be more like a friendly game of scrabble. The praise it earns him in stopping the behaviour will become more desirable than the behaviour itself, but our dog then needs to test it out, to be sure that the same behaviour will be dealt with in exactly the same manner. This testing period can last for anything up to 20 minutes and our perseverance and consistency is essential throughout. See it as showing and teaching our dog the confidence to react differently to a situation, rather than stopping the responses that our dog has been programmed to perform.

Also, interrupting from the same position continually is not advised – we need to step to new position each time. We must also remember that this is an *instant* interruption, A CHINK, not an annoying jingle jingle jingle. Just one chink, followed by immediate prolonged non-physical praise). Oh, and another point: eliminate any other similar sounds – **tape up any discs on the collar that chink!**

Most Common Problems:
Inconsistency:
a) One person in the family is doing their best to train using 'sound distraction' techniques and others are refusing to follow suite. This will confuse the dog, cause conflict and reduce trust and respect.
b) Even if everyone in the family uses 'sound distraction', some fail to use the technique every-time. This can, and probably will, create a negative response.

Lack of Confidence:
Belief that this will not be enough to stop the undesirable behaviour. This

creates a tendency to panic, and use an undesirable alternative (yelling, grabbing dog, pulling on lead etc.). The inconsistency will confuse the dog, and reduce trust.

Giving up:
Interrupting behaviour once or twice, using 'sound distraction', thinking it isn't working and trying something else before the learning process has taken place and the technique has had chance to be effective. For example, Dog Barking:

a) — Interrupt behaviour with one chink of the keys, followed by immediate non-physical praise.

b) Dog WILL stop barking when s/he first hears the sound, even if you can't see/hear it (this is what we're praising – STOPPING).

c) Then s/he starts to bark again: –

d) We repeat, exactly as (a) above), but from a different position. (results in (b) above)

e) Dog starts barking again: –

f) We repeat 'exactly' as (a) above), different position again. (results in (b) above)

g) Dog starts barking again:–

h) We give up and yell at dog. Consequence: nothing learned, dog's won the battle, and sees no advantage in stopping the behaviour we're addressing.

Additional Sounds that distort the effect:
Other chink and jingle sounds coming from the collar discs. We should tape together anything on the collar or lead that clatters, chinks or jingles. We should also remember the sound needs to be just one precise chink, not an annoying jingle.

Recap - Interrupting Behaviour with Sound, and Experiment

Once our dog is efficiently 'key-sound conditioned' to come to us, (see page 10, and SoundPlay Classroom), the same sound can be used to interrupt any undesirable behaviour. This would be appropriate for barking, yelping, howling, messing, digging, growling, puppy nipping, mouthing, getting up on the furniture, emptying the waste bin. It's important though, that the sound of the keys or chinx, interrupting the behaviour is always followed by prolonged verbal praise. We don't wait/pause for the behaviour to stop before praising – the instant praise associated with the sound is what draws the dog's attention away from the behaviour (once conditioned that is). Far better in my opinion to distract (and praise for stopping) than to yell 'No'. Please trust me - by praising immediately after the sound distraction, we're 'not' praising for the behaviour we wish to stop. Yelling continually at pup will create anxiety – he really hasn't a clue what he's doing so wrong. Let's face it, our children take years to learn what we expect pup to know in just a few short weeks!!! Often it's our lack of patience, and hasty reprimands that creates the problem behaviours in the first place. For Sound Distraction to work, we need to condition our dog to the sound. I design conditioning exercises almost daily – once you've tried a few you may find yourself de-signing your own. Some will suit you and your dog better than others. The aim is always to 'attract and excite' our dog. At the point of highest excite-ment, we introduce the sound, then 'immediately' praise. Let's set up an experiment... You'll need a little cheese and a set of keys. *(Also, before this experiment can be introduced, please address 'Nipping and Mouthing' - Page 32).* Divide the cheese into 6 small pieces. Hold one piece only in clenched hand (hold keys in other hand). Move hand with cheese (still clenched) towards dog and allow him to pick up the scent. Then, move both hands behind your back. Now.... timing is crucial – the keys have to chink **once** only, **'as'** you praise **'as'** you bring hand forward again and feed your dog. Repeat 5 times. Half hour or so later, chink keys once and praise your dog ... if your timing was good in the experiment, your dog should stop whatever he's doing and come to you. This is all very well, but unless we feed our dog every time we chink, the effects may soon diminish... that's why SoundPlay doesn't use food as reward.

Separation Anxiety

Sometimes behaviours such as chewing, howling and general destructive-ness while out, can be the result of **separation anxiety or over attachment.** Most of us enjoy the unconditional love, friendship and blind loyalty we receive from our dog. However along with this goes 'dependence' where in some dogs the bond becomes so excessive that the dog is insecure and panics when left alone. This can also be the case with adopted dogs who've found a good home, (perhaps for the first time in their life), where they are shown love and fairness – they can become afraid it will all suddenly stop and therefore become anxious when we're not there.

It's important we identify this behaviour with anxiety and insecurity and **not** with wilful destructiveness or bad behaviour. **Punishment and reprimand**

can increase the anxiety and create a worsening situation. Is your dog showing signs of jealousy, over-protectiveness, chewing while away, excessive barking/whining, always coming between you and your partner/another dog? Sometimes (but not always) it's necessary to detach oneself a little and show less affection to our dog. This is extremely difficult and we must be sure this is the correct solution in our particular situation before choosing this route. However, if you feel you are doing too much of the following, it's likely to be the case.

◆ **Is our Dog sleeping constantly on laps and then perhaps also on our bed throughout the night?**
   If so, we must create a rest place for him (his own bed – somewhere that's ' his own place'). Call this 'bed'. Leave him there from time to time, while at home – somewhere away from us – a conservatory, hallway, place under the stairs. Have a rug and water bowl there. Say 'bed' every time we direct him to the spot. Also, leave a favourite toy by the bed (biscuit ball or Kong).

◆ **Are we responding to <u>every</u> approach by our dog with conversation, a stroke, fondling of the ears, or throwing a ball?** *If so, we must make such pleasures occasional rather than constant. If our dog, for instance, approaches us wanting to play, ignore him; then, after 10 minutes or so, once our dog's forgotten his invitation or demand, perhaps WE invite him to play. We then become the initiator, thus building our dog's sense of security.*

◆ **Are we making too much an event, when we return home.** (Fussing or reprimanding over a mess, or apologising for being away so long, or even greeting our dog before saying 'hello' to other members of the family). *If so, we must ignore our dog for a couple of minutes when first arriving home – keep busy, putting shopping away, changing clothes, or making a cup of tea, or saying 'hello' to people first. After a few minutes, we say 'hello' to our dog.*

◆ We must NEVER make an issue of destructive behaviour – it'll increase anxiety and make a re-occurrence more likely.

Having identified the destructive behaviour as being 'separation anxiety', it's important we don't leave our dog longer than his tolerance limit. Also, we don't allow anticipation that we'll be gone for long periods every time we go out (we have found it better to leave for short periods, and return as though we've forgotten something - then, leave again). Perhaps give our dog something with our scent to keep company while we're out. Say 'goodbye' (a consistent verbal signal) every time we go out (e.g. 'back soon') -

this is a great way to build security – especially if we do this every time we walk out the door, and particularly if we return a few times before actually leaving.

Here's a suggestion:

1. While preparing yourself for going out, maintain pleasant disposition – **Don't** show signs of anxiety, e.g. 'Oh, I'm late, it's all your fault – everything has to be out of reach, because of your chewing – you'd better not make a mess today my lad.'
2. Once ready..... say 'Okay Fido, be a good boy. BACK SOON.'
3. Go to dog's place (bed) and pick up your dog's toy - say nothing – return toy to bed – say nothing, and depart.
4. Walk to car – back again – back indoors – ignore dog while you enter – go to dog's bed – praise dog while standing by bed.
5. Walk into another room as if you've forgotten something.
6. Repeat departure as 2 & 3 above and remember how to behave when finally returning home.

'Association Learning'

Ever heard 'That rings a bell'? Something that triggers an association with something we remember, something we see, smell, hear, feel or read. Let's explore 'sounds'. We hear the sound of a fire engine siren – we associate this with distress. This sound will distract us even be it, for a split second and at that split second we feel anxious. We hear sounds every day that we associate to things that have happened in the past. Sometimes we barely notice it, but at others it can effect our mood all day. That amazing love song, meant so much to us long ago – we haven't heard it for years - played on the radio this morning – just can't get it out of our mind - brings back so many memories). It can work with dogs too. How do most dogs respond when we open a tin of dog food? If we could get that response any time of day, we'd have our dog's constant attention! Our dog doesn't need to understand how we open the tin, to know the sound means 'food's a-comin'. This is why 'treat' training works with dogs. However, we don't always have treats with us, we can't be sure our dog's always hungry enough for food to be significantly attractive, and there's the risk that the dog will put on too much weight if we depend on rewarding with food all the time. Yes, food is important to the dog, but I believe there's something far more satisfying to most dogs: the 'chase and capture', the 'recognition or worth', and the 'respect of the pack'. **Strengthening the pack and survival of the species.** Canines are one of the few species that will hunt animals larger than themselves. Wild dogs work to 'strengthen the pack' and in so doing, ensure survival of their species. Hunting down and capturing large prey is essential in their practice and strengthening. Showing weaknesses could mean abandonment by the rest of the pack. Only newcomers strong enough can join the pack. This could be why we sometimes mistake dogs 'show of worth' with aggression. The 'desire' to hunt is in all dogs, but for most domesticated dogs, this desire is suppressed. If we can simulate the hunt, with play, and at the same time introduce a 'sound association', we should find this more effective than a can of dog food being opened. In order that a sound is truly effective as a distraction, we need to 'condition' our dog to associate that sound with something more attractive and pleasing than anything else. Timing, body language, and voice control, is essential. Level of success, is determined by the quality, consistency and determination of the handling. Dr. Ivan Pavlov discovered conditioned reflex in the first decade of this century. It's written that he came upon this discovery quite by accident while working with some dogs in an experiment for human psychology. He noticed that some dogs began to drool, even prior to entering the research laboratory, in anticipation of food rewards that they'd grown to expect during his experiment. This aggravated his curiosity to the point that he needed to see what was going on. A selection of dogs were allocated for further investigation. No doubt, you have heard of "Pavlov's' bell". If not, perhaps the expression "that rings a bell". That's where we believe it comes from. The dogs were presented with some food while a bell was struck. After several occasions of this conditioning, the bell was struck without the promised treat. The dogs naturally got excited anticipating the food reward, and began to salivate (drool). Hence, the discovery of conditioned reflex. Conditioning, means the same stimuli, presented in the same exact manner, which will create a reflex, (a reaction) that one has no control over. Unfortunately, it's possible to condition a dog by fear, and seemingly obtain an effective response (the sound and pain of a check collar for instance). The problem with this technique is that with some dogs it can backfire, and teach the dog that the only way to avoid the pain is to fight back. Hence, aggression. In order to undo the harm, we have to modify the dog's perception of the sound of the check collar, and convince him that there'll be no further pain. (Loose lead training – see page 49).

'Dog Direction' - Let's go to work !!

Let's consider our relationship with our dogs in a whole new perspective. Realistically, we're not strictly speaking training, as the dog already achieves all the postures and behaviours the average pet owner aims to teach (Walk, Sit, Stay, Down, Run, Come, Fetch, Touch, Drop, Speak/Silence). We perhaps should aim for, 'identification/organisation' - setting the rules for the when's and where's, rather than the do's and don'ts. We know dogs love to work, so let's move away from thinking 'dog training', and move towards 'dog directing'. Working as a pack/family/work force, together, as a team. Imagine humans being directors, running the home as, say a business, with our dog taking up position as manager. If we see the opportunity, or the need, we can work anywhere – we're freelance. Firstly, we have to make clear what we're offering and what we expect, in return *(Trust, Stability, Justice, Reliability, Confidence, Appreciation and Consistency)*. Secondly, we have to discuss the Contract of Employment *(Socialisation, Sound-Conditioning & Pack Exercises)*. Thirdly, we have to give them the privileges they deserve. Although we of course have to delegate, we allow them the power of thought, and the initiative to follow their own instincts. Additionally, as our working day may be full, we have to allow free time where relaxation and socialisation can take place, for all. Some of the work we do may be vital to the smooth running of the company. We therefore have to always be seen as honest, fair, competent, reliable, and consistent, especially when our intervention be required. Our dog can then trust enough that he can sit back and/or respond, as guided, while we do our part of the job. E.g. 'Recall' and 'Stay'. Our work is such that we need to design verbal and physical key 'directions', to avoid confusion and time loss. Most commonly used words to direct a behaviour: **Gently, Heel, Loose, Sit, Straight-Sit, Stay, Come, Down, Hold, Give, Off, Jump, Speak, Quiet & Wait.** To 'teach' the meanings of each word, and clearly identify the action required, we must say it 'only when our dog is actually 'exhibiting the action' or 'in the position'. Once our dog understands the word we can then use it to 'direct' our dog. Sound Distraction can be used to 'distract from a behaviour', (to get our dog's attention), and to call our dog back to us. In order to teach the words and 'condition to the sound interruption' we must consider the following:

◆ *Consistent, well-timed and accurate hand & body language.*
◆ *Clear and precise allocation of voice sounds - always followed by praise (exceptions: stay and wait).*
◆ *Preconditioned effective use of Sound Tool.*
◆ *The ability to work together as a team, with mutual trust and respect.*

Puppies first encounter with the lead

Most of us assume that a lead to a puppy is like a harness to a toddler – but it isn't ! Should I wish to compare it to anything, my child's first inoculation comes to mind. When our puppy first comes home he needs to wear an identity collar. This new experience can cause anxiety to our pup, but usually it's not long before he forgets about it. We have to be careful not to buckle it too tight, and make sure we check it at least once a week to allow for growth.

Then the lead – it's crucial that we introduce the lead in a kind and painless manner. We're perhaps conditioned to thinking dogs walk naturally on leads, but to the dog, it defies nature to be tied in anyway.

An improper introduction to the lead can cause anxiety and problems in the future. We must be sure this collar our pup has learned to trust doesn't suddenly cause pain, and the pup therefore sees us as one to be feared and not trusted.

A suggestion: First, we find come knitting wool, or sewing cotton – 5 - 7 ft long. Take collar off and tie one end of wool/cotton to the collar. Put collar back on puppy. We stay with pup, but don't hold the wool for at least 5 minutes. Watch to make sure pup doesn't eat the wool, or tie himself up. Find a toy and play fetch – calling as little attention to the wool as possible. After a few minutes, pick up and hold the other end of the wool while continuing play for a further 5 – 10 mins. If the space between pup and us extends so the wool becomes taught, drop the wool immediately. We need to repeat this several times a day for a few days. Then the same, but with a light lead.

After the play session, we can leave the lead dragging on pup for half an hour or so, but keep pup in sight. If pup shows signs of anxiety, we must reduce the time he's dragging the lead. Only after pup is happy with a lead attached to his collar should we think about walking him on lead. We must take care and never allow the lead to become tight. Tension on his neck can inhibit his ability to think and listen, and will usually cause resistance - he'll pull away.

Pup's first heel lesson

Before we walk pup, we need teach him what "heel" means – the word's just a meaningless sound to pup at the moment. We must teach him to identify the sound with a position beside our left leg, moving in rhythm to it.

Saying heel, once pup has moved out of position is in fact teaching "don't heel – race off". Pup will race off farther and farther, thinking this is what we want – perhaps pulling harder and harder wondering why it's never hard enough – ("IT HURTS! Why do they want me to hurt - this is madness").

We can start to teach heel from a stationery position. Position pup beside our left leg and say "Heel" - IMMEDIATELY praise and move forward taking small bouncy paces - keep praising. We want pup to try and catch up with us. If it's not fun, he'll have no time for it. Once he's caught up, say 'heel' - keep feet moving and about turn. If we keep him keen, he'll chase again - he won't be able to resist. Continue like this repeating the word 'heel' every time pup arrives in position. Should he race on too far, we STOP and say nothing – **when** he realises the game's stopped and looks back for more, we praise him for paying attention, but we **don't** say heel, because he's not **at** heel. The words confirm the meaning, so the doing has to be as the word is used – not after or before.

No matter how enjoyable this is to pup, he'll eventually become bored – we learn to notice the signs and finish the heel-game before this happens. When we feel it's time to stop, we give a 'release':- something like, 'Okay then – that's it', clap hands playfully, rumble tumble play for a couple of minutes as we praise, praise, praise.   Exercise over.

Socialisation and Environment

Some 15-20% (possibly more) dogs have a fear or apprehension of some description. The causes could range from people, other animals or even a place/situation. How many times have we heard: *My dog doesn't like men, doesn't like the vet, doesn't like being groomed. He's fine with animals except cows and sheep. I can't take my dog to town - he doesn't like crowded places,* and so on.

In most cases this can be traced back to between birth and about 16 weeks of age, and shouldn't be confused with behavioural problems related to cruelty or bad training procedures. This is why it's so important to properly socialise our pup immediately.

A puppy becomes aware of its social/environmental surroundings at about 3 weeks old (or earlier) and even whilst still with the litter we should, if possible start to address the problem. Apprehension and anxiety can be triggered by sight, scent, touch, and sound.

People: Some pups appear more comfortable with women. The chances are that the litter was predominately raised by the lady of the house with only a small amount of interaction, if any, by men. Generally, once pup arrives home, it's we women who care for pup throughout the greater part of the day. Pup will undoubtedly become accustomed to 'Dad', but may not be too sure about other men. We need to invite plenty of couples round, take pup to places where men frequent, and encourage pup to accept these two legged giants are harmless.

Other Animals: If we live in the city, we rarely see cows, pigs, sheep etc. Keep in mind that unless we introduce other animals to our pup early on, he may fear them or see them as prey once mature.

What do we do? Once we've chosen our pup, visit him regularly and ask that we can interact with him as much as possible prior to collection. Aim to take pup home at the earliest possible safe stage, (the younger the better). Begin a socialisation strategy immediately - even though pup isn't fully vaccinated until 10-12 weeks old it's possible to invite friends home to meet him. As many types as possible: all age groups (babies to the older generation), gents, ladies, short, tall, large and small. Introduce pup to the postman and anyone who wears a uniform or a hat.

Take pup out in the car (see travelling): town, parks, farms, train stations, airports, pubs - carry your pup with you. Frequent use of the vacuum cleaner, turn on the radio — the more we do the better. An almost endless list, even before vaccination is completed. Once pup is vaccinated, take him to puppy socialisation classes. Soundplay Email: classroom@soundplaydogs.com

Puppy is very wary: We'll no doubt find our pup is more apprehensive about some things than others. We must not overreact. Too much reassurance can reinforce pup's fear. Better to show this new thing hasn't affected us in any way — we must lead by example. If pup's fearful of a specific, introduce this perceived threat, as often as possible, but from a distance and each time gradually closer as the response improves. Always positive and confident - rewarding pup with verbal praise each time he doesn't react or when he recovers from the new, fearful experience.

Early Introduction Checklist: People of all ages: beards, glasses, walking sticks, all shapes and sizes. People in different clothing, uniforms, hats, crash helmets etc; people running, jogging, dancing, singing, laughing or just talking loudly; as many dogs as possible from a tiny Jack Russell to giant Great Danes, all ages whether one at a time or in a group. Also, cats, rabbits, birds, sheep, cows, horses etc. Introduce a collar and lead as soon as possible. (See 'First time on the lead', Page 22). Groom pup every day (see Page 26 & 36).

To prevent traumatic vet visits, practise mock health examinations - checking gums and teeth, lifting paws, stroke and massage various different areas of pup's body. Other people can do this too, but best you're always present. Watch that children don't tease pup or grab him accidentally - pups will mimic and learn to play rough, if so taught. Frequent short rides in the car; 3 daily 5-minute drives are better than a single two hour drive once a week. Slowly accustom pup to unexpected loud noises — vacuum cleaner, lawn mower, washing machine, electric drill etc.

Jumping Up

Teaching 'Stand' to stop Jumping Up

Most dogs love being groomed – we can teach our dog the word 'stand' while grooming and thereafter say 'Stand' to prevent jumping up. It's so simple, yet so effective. There's a wonderful grooming product on the market that grooms, massages and discards dry skin: The Zoom Groom by 'Kong' – Dogs love it !!! Another way is to teach the difference between 'jump' and 'stand'. Encourage dog to jump, say 'jump'.... When dog lands, say 'stand'.

In order to reach our mouth, our dog needs to jump up. If we consider that instinctively, wild dogs will seek out what the returning hunting dog has brought back for them **in their mouth,** and that the desire is overwhelming, we can appreciate how ineffective and unkind reprimand would be to stop this natural gesture of greeting. Once our dog knows there's nothing to share, s/he will go back along their way. Yelling, pushing, kicking, kneeing, can create more serious problems, and discourage our dog from **coming back to us**, when called. Although we may feel privileged that our dog accepts us as the hunting dog, it can be annoying, especially if wearing our best outfit! There's a couple of ways we've found effective in stopping dogs jumping up. When entering the house (keys in hand), drop keys to floor directly in front of dog, just as s/he's thinking about jumping up. Attention will be diverted downwards to the sound of keys hitting floor. Bend down to eye level, greet dog, stand and walk away.

Other times: If dog jumps up at other times, cross arms to opposite shoulder, turn and walk away. Say nothing. **Never** Say 'down', reprimand or push dog down or away:

We never reprimand our dog for jumping up – this will teach our dog not to come to us. We have found that this can make re-call training far more difficult. Also it can severely damage the dog's natural play drive, which can lead to an inability to interact naturally and the possibility of aggressive or mounting behaviour later on.

Jumping up at visitors: This problem needs to be addressed before visitor enters our home. We need to teach our dog to remain on all four feet when interacting with people: Let's discuss what we are really teaching our dog -

> Question: What position would we prefer our dog were in when greeting people?
> Answer: Standing firm on all four legs.
> Conclusion: Teach dog to understand 'Stand'.

Groom & Stand Exercise: Walk dog into a stand: gently hold the under-collar with left hand, guide dog forward into a standing position. Groom with right hand, while saying 'Stand - good dog'....'Stand, - good dog'..... (again and again). Continue for several minutes. Should the dog move out of the stand position (sit or lay for instance), we **stop grooming immediately, and say nothing**. The reward of grooming only occurs while our dog remains standing. Every time the dog moves out of the stand position, we silently walk him back into a stand and start grooming again.

If we repeat this exercise several times a day for a week, our dog will soon learn to 'stand' when asked.

Thereafter, anytime our dog attempts to jump up at us, we instantly take a couple of quick paces back (away from dog) and say 'stand', **as** dog falls to the stand position.

We have found this method ideal for curing jumping up! Once our dog understands the word 'stand', we can instruct our dog to 'stand' (to be on four legs), whenever he jumps up onto two legs. 'Stand' is useful for vets visits too. Please note: While still **teaching** our dog a position, we must take care to only say the appropriate word while our dog's **in** that position.

Feeding & Begging

Feeding: I've found that with many dogs showing behaviour problems, changing their diet can significantly improve the situation. Red meat is high in protein and can cause a dog to become hyperactive – Most tinned food is an expensive way of feeding our dog with high quantities of fluid (water), and wheat can be guilty of many side effects. I prefer to feed my dogs boiled rice with chicken, tripe or white fish. Most reputable pet stores have a good range of frozen meats for pets. We need to add vitamins and minerals, (buy from your vets or a good pet store) and also a little sunflower oil. For dogs that prefer biscuits, my advice is to buy rice based, rather than wheat.

Begging: It's generally agreed that, in the dog world, those higher up the ladder eat first. I don't necessarily eat before my dogs, but never have a problem with them begging. We need to set the rules right from the start:

- We never feed a dog from our plate, or while eating at the table (No matter how cute he looks, or how annoying he becomes – **ignore him**)
- We don't feed our dogs the scraps as soon as we've finished eating (if our dog thinks us eating means treats will follow, he'll be drooling all through our meal)
- Be firm with children and visitors - no, we don't feed our dog from the table – ever!
- Yelling won't help – be consistent and follow the above rules.
- If all else fails – fill his Kong tightly with rice and chicken mix and let him chew on it while you eat.
- Food for thought: Do we make eating too easy. Perhaps civilisation creates a certain amount of boredom for this hunting, prey catching species? In the wild, dogs have to work for their food. (See digging, page 37). Ideally, we should hide our dogs food – let them work for it – never give it them 'on a plate'. The desire to steal, search, ransack would then perhaps be fulfilled and a lot of those unwanted behaviours extinguished.

Travelling in the Car

Sickness & Panic: First let's explore why our puppy/dog is anxious, sick or both when travelling in the car. If we go back to the very first time s/he was in the car it was probably either the first time s/he was separated from Mum, or on the first trip to the vet's. Both extremely traumatic! Therefore our pup is not too keen on repeating the experience (for every bad memory we need 100 good ones to compensate). So don't add to them by dragging puppy to the car or yelling at him when he's sick. Let's instead get cracking on these good experiences s/he can associate with our car in the future.

◆ Play with him on the way to the car.

◆ Don't make a big deal about getting into the car.

◆ Locate a park or field **near** home and travel there by car for a good game of fetch.

◆ Don't feed puppy for at least an hour before a car trip.

◆ Give you car a check up – look for shocks, excessive noise, fumes or heat *(All these things can exacerbate carsickness in anyone, not only dogs).*

◆ Desensitise your dog:

(Sit him in the car with the motor OFF. Carefully time how long he is comfortable before you notice him start to drool, or show signs of being uncomfortable).

Then when you do take him out in the car never go over that time.

Test the time once a week and you should be able to slowly increase journey lengths.

The majority of dogs who are anxious about car travel never get to the point where they refuse to get in one. They will however, pant anxiously throughout the journey and even salivate copiously, which is a physiological response to anxiety, as is vomiting. What if the vomiting is a physical response to the movement of the car, in the same way as sea sickness is induced by the movement of a boat? The nausea is triggered by the movement of fluids in the inner ear. If this is the problem, medication may be required. If you suspect that travel sickness rather than anxiety is the difficulty, it would be wise to discuss the matter with your vet.

No – he still won't get in the car!

Try this, but make sure you have plenty of time to spare and you have to be patient! Opening both rear passenger doors and then with your dog on a long lead, climb in and don't look back. The lead may be a little taught, but don't pull hard and don't allow lead to become tight. **Remain absolutely silent.** Slowly crawl to other side of car and get out the other door (hide and remain silent – keep lead taught but don't tug or pull and make sure puppy is not in discomfort) - your dog will eventually have to get in. When it does, continue to look away from puppy and lots of praise. Puppy will follow you out of the car. Run round to first door and repeat over and over again. Puppy will soon think it's a game and get so excited that he'll probably try to jump in before you after a while – at which point you close the second door behind you and sit in the back seat with puppy for a short while. Next time (taking care not to ruin everything by letting him feel trapped) – open the door quickly and start over again. You can gradually increase the time you spend sitting in the back seat.

Once puppy is happy sitting in the back seat with you, you can climb over to the front seat and take him for a very short spin – to the park. If he panics when the engine starts, turn it off and call it a day – use your own judgement here. You may have to play the game a few times with variations. Remember though – don't lose your temper with him and don't yell.

Housetraining

It's important that we always remember that our puppies are not misbehaving when they have accidents indoors – it's partly because of their previous environment, and also because they simply don't have adequate control. **We should never scold our pup.** Scolding will cause endless problems in the future. Our pup can become so confused and afraid to go, that he'll only feel safe going when we're not around. Then, no matter how many times we take puppy out he'll not want to be seen doing something we've taught him is 'bad'. He'll hold on until back indoors and we're out of sight (some puppies and even badly trained adult dogs will hide every time they want to go and we'll find packages under and behind furniture everywhere). If the scolding continues, s/he will soon suffer from anxiety and develop numerous behavioural problems as a result – chewing, barking, yelping, nipping, etc. etc. We never rub our dog's nose in it! Apart from being cruel, it creates a constant scent that encourages rather than discourages the behaviour. How, then, do we deal with it? If we can catch pup in the act we pick up gently by the scruff and silently trot outside, and gently place pup on the ground. Then we wait, and hope pup continue. Immediately he does, we say a word that we'll use to identify 'going' (say, loo loo) and then immediately praise. Chewing and exercise often stimulates the urge to go. We can take pup out for a good romp before we retire - encourage chewing and play fetch. If we can encourage excited passing before we retire, it'll be less likely there'll be accidents during the night.

We shouldn't feed puppy too late – 5 hours or so before we retire. Reduce amount of water during the evening (we should of course always ensure puppy has water, but we need not fill the bowl before retiring).

Also we can clean the area thoroughly – our vets are usually up to date with safe cleaning products. In days gone by we used ammonia from the local hardware store, but it's highly toxic and it really shouldn't be used while animals or children are around – the fumes are dangerous. So, best we choose a safe product that will neutralise all smells. Then put something over the area where accidents have occurred - a chair or a basket. Scents will then be gone and the area no longer be available (we shouldn't cover the area with newspaper, this will only encourage more accidents).

Teaching our dog where to go – **every** time puppy goes outside, **as s/he begins to go** give a verbal signal (e.g: 'loo loo') and then immediately praise. Assuming there are no medical problems, it is probably just a matter of puppy adjusting to a new routine. We pay no attention to accidents, unless we catch during the act (see above).

Barking!

Excessive Barking - someone's at the door:

It's great to know that our dog will alert us if there's a potential intruder outside – especially if the visitor's close to the windows and doors. I'll always praise my dogs for doing a fine job when this happens. However, there are dogs that become anxious about intruders and have somehow failed to learn when they can relax to allow us the responsibility of analysing the situation once their duty's done. It helps if we can think in terms of 'a job' – if, like me, we accept all or at least most things dogs do as 'working'. Thus we simply need to identify signals and sounds that represent task instructions. Of course, we need to be consistent: work is a serious business!

'Speak'/'Quiet': One way to befriend the neighbours is to teach our dog the word 'Quiet'. However, our dog needs to understand what 'Quiet' means. Imagine an on/off switch: 'Speak' (on) = 'bark' and 'Quiet' (off) = 'no bark'. We understand the words but dogs don't, so first we associate the sound 'Speak' with the action of barking: we need to say the word as our dog is barking, but we also need to initiate the bark. Teasing with a toy, or food is good. Immediately and **as** our dog barks, we say 'Speak, good dog.' Immediately our dog stops barking (pauses for breath between barks), we say 'Quiet, good dog', and give the toy (reward is, of course, the best motivation). After a while, our dog will learn to bark when we say 'Speak', and stop barking, when we say 'Quiet'.

Incessant Barking: A dog that incessantly barks when left alone could be suffering from **Separation Anxiety** and believes calling out will bring the pack home. (See Page 17)

Barking in the garden: Most dogs will bark to chase people or other dogs away from our home territory, and although we think the intruder is long gone, our dog can scent and hear him far longer than we can. Perhaps we should consider this and realise they need to 'finish the job properly', instead of yelling at them for what we see as unnecessary barking. From their viewpoint it could appear that we're not happy with their efforts and need to help along side by yelling/barking louder than them. The result may be that next time they will aim to do the job better – and louder – and for longer!!!

Scientists have discovered that dogs have a primitive language of their own. By varying degrees of growling, whining, barking and grunting sounds, they are able to communicate around 40 different meanings. By varying the tone and manner of these sounds they are able to communicate aggression, defensiveness, and a variety of needs and emotions. Although these sounds are a necessary part of a dog's vocabulary the most frequently used, barking, can cause problems, both to ourselves and our neighbours. We want our dogs to act as guard dogs and warn off or alert us to possible intruders but we forget that they are unable to distinguish between these and legitimate visitors approaching the house. In the latter case we usually end up shouting at the dog to silence it, whereupon the dog interprets this shouting as a form of barking. It assumes that we are joining in and, finding its actions apparently confirmed, barks louder, happy that it is pleasing us by doing what it mistakenly thinks we require of it.

Dogs bark for other reasons, the most common being to communicate a desire for attention. Again, we frequently shout at them to stop, failing to realise that this may be, to the dog, a form of attention. Thus we inadvertently reinforce the very behavioural problem we wish to correct.

This form of barking frequently manifests itself when the dog sees that the owner's attention is centred elsewhere, perhaps in conversation with another person, reading a newspaper or, most irritating of all, trying to concentrate on driving the car. The best cure for attention seeking barking, is to ignore it. If you get up and leave the room, or turn your back, or simply remain silent the dog will eventually learn that barking gets no response and is counter-productive.

Nipping & Mouthing

Puppy Biting (Bite Inhibition)

Watching a litter of puppies playing, we'll see they have great fun biting and grabbing each other with their mouths. This is normal puppy behaviour –

oral gratification, communication, and a sign of 'friendship'. When we take a puppy from the litter and into our home, s/he will miss this interaction and long to play bite and mouth us (his/her new pack) – still a sign of 'friendship'. (and BONDING) This is normal, inevitable, essential behaviour, but needs to be modified – a compromise is in order so that we and our children don't get sore.

One of the first thing to teach our new puppy is that human flesh is much more sensitive than puppies who wear a fur coat, and that it can be painful when they bite. (although they're only playing, we need to explain to them our situation). Therefore, we teach our puppy 'bite inhibition', but without distorting the 'bite reflex'. A puppy has very sharp teeth and a weak jaw. Therefore, nipping and mouthing is uncomfortable, but can rarely cause severe damage. An adult dog has duller teeth and a powerful jaw, and capable of causing significant damage when biting. This is why we have to teach our pup to 'soft grip – gently' when playing/mouthing, **rather than** 'no mouthing at all - biting isn't allowed.' The exercise is essential for when s/he becomes adult. If they haven't been taught the difference, the first bite, when adult could be fatal.

GIVEN CERTAIN CIRCUMSTANCES, ANY DOG WILL BITE!

If a small child falls on our adult dog and sticks a finger in its eye, we shouldn't be surprised if the dog bites. If we do a good job teaching our puppy bite inhibition, we'll still get the growl and the grab, but should get a grab and release without damage. If we don't, we may get a hard bite with significant damage.

It's simple to teach a puppy bite inhibition. Every time the puppy touches us with its teeth, say "OUCH!" in a surprised firm tone of voice. Quickly place left hand on right shoulder, and visa versa – ignore pup until there's a break in the mouthing, or the mouthing turns to a lick, then praise. (Repeat a few times if necessary). This will probably not stop the puppy from mouthing, but over time should result in softer and gentler puppy biting. **Squealing and teasing children don't help to solve the problem. We have to teach them to behave as we wish our pup to behave (dogs mimic)!** Some puppies are overly active with mouthing and nipping. If that's the case, we do the following:

Teaching a puppy to be gentle: Hold in clenched hand some cooked chicken or cheese. Say 'HOLD' in soothing tone and allow pup to find just one small piece of the chicken. Then close the remaining in hand and say "GENTLY" in that same soothing tone but more drawn out. Keep hand close to pup's mouth, still clenched. If puppy touches hand at all, repeat 'GENTLY' and withdraw hand right away from pup's mouth (behind your back). Wait a few seconds, then move hand back towards pup's mouth. Say 'Gently' (*with* *immediate praise).*

Here's the important part: IF pup touches hand, withdraw immediately, saying 'GENTLY' again. However, IF/WHEN pup doesn't touch hand say 'HOLD' and allow him to seek another piece of food (just one). If pup snatches, say 'GENTLY' and withdraw hand again. Pup learns that not touching is rewarded with food, whereas touching, or snatching results in no food. After a short while, you'll probably have your pup sitting and waiting attentively for your invitation to take the next piece of chicken. Thereafter, we can use the verbal sound 'GENTLY' to mean 'don't touch', and 'HOLD' for picking an article up in his/her mouth (can be used when playing 'fetch' for instance). We can do this exercise with the puppy before meals when attentiveness is at highest.

Thereafter:

a. Unexpected mouthing (you don't know the puppy is going to mouth, until you feel the puppy's teeth):

Say 'OUCH!'

b. Expected mouthing (you see the puppy getting ready to mouth you):

Say 'Gently' before the puppy can mouth you – immediately praise.

c. The puppy is mouthing you because of a desire to play'

You have to answer the question, 'Do I have time to play with the puppy now ?" If you do, it's important that pup thinks it's you that's initiated the play, not him. Walk away from pup, collect play toys from toy-box, return to pup and introduce play –"'fetch' is good.

If the answer is 'No, I don't have time for the puppy, right now,' either walk away from puppy and ignore behaviour or put puppy in place s/he sleeps with a chew toy for a while.

Toys, Teething & Play

Toys: To a puppy, everything is a toy and needs to be played with, chewed, and if possible, even swallowed: the end of his tail, a waving pencil, the novel you've been reading for weeks, his own droppings, legs of our best dining table, carpets (doesn't matter if they're old or new), electric cables, poisonous plants, dirty rusty old cans found in the garden, dead birds, frogs, mice – video cameras, computer mouse, electronic organisers, telephone cables, handles of carving knives, babies nappies, our best shoes, and so on. If our puppy has access to these things quite frankly, it's as much our fault as if we gave a toddler access. Yes, it's difficult! Life with a puppy isn't always as enchanting as we thought before s/he arrived. Our whole life pattern has to change (as with a new baby). We know our puppy needs to chew and play – so we set up a nursery, 3 or 4 safe toys to play with, **and we never reprimand pup for chewing the wrong toy!**

Which toys are safe? When choosing our puppy's toys, beware of the dangers:

Small Balls: - A small bouncy rubber ball present a potentially serious danger where it can form a close-fitting plug in the dog's oesophagus and choke him within minutes – even tennis balls have been known to cause asphyxiation.

Foam filled toys are especially dangerous since their contents can be swallowed and cause intestinal blockage as they expand in the stomach.

Wooden sticks can splinter, and should <u>never</u> be thrown for a dog – they've been known to cause horrible mouth, eye, ear, throat injuries this way.

Nylon chews: Synthetic nylon has been moulded into an assortment of shapes like bones, balls and Frisbees, and some dogs love to chew them if they are also prone to chewing other hard objects such as stones. However, because nylon lacks elasticity and does not bounce, most dogs find it boring. Nylon toys should never be thrown as they can induce slab fractures when grabbed at speed.

Ropes: Rough ropes made from the natural fibres of flax and cotton can make excellent toys for dogs. Unlike nylon, these natural products can be digested and cleared from the dog's gut if swallowed accidentally and they permit penetration of the teeth and massage the gums. The loose, tufted ends of commercially made rope toys stimulate the same shake-kill action as when a wolf tears into its prey. Also, there is some evidence that these ropes can function along the lines of dental floss, polishing the surface of the tooth and dislodging organic plaque and food debris.

Bones: Unless specifically advised (Great Danes, etc) we would recommend you never feed your dog bones. Apart from the splintering, the ground bone can form masses in the dog's stomach.

Kong, Kong Biscuit Balls*, and *Cool Kong on a Rope – These are wonderful toys for pups and dogs. Safe and pleasurable. The ordinary Kong and the Biscuit Ball are good for teething and separation anxiety. Cool Kong on a rope is wonderful for playing fetch and teaching 'down'.

All Kong products, the Halti, Zoom Groom and SoundPlay Chinx can be purchased from SoundPlay Dogs: accessories@soundplaydogs.com

Other Toys: If you're not absolutely sure about a toy being safe, don't give it to your dog – for instance, sweetcorn husks are a particular common cause of gastro-intestinal blockage to dogs, and there are many more potential dangers from plastic, nylon, bone, wood and stone.

Play: Once we have decided what goes into your puppy's toy-box, we need to teach pup that these are his to play with. Simply play with pup with the chosen toys (indoor fetch is a great game for this) – always start by taking them from the toy-box and always finish by returning them to the toy-box after playtime. Always take pup outside after play time as this is when he is most likely to need to relieve himself.

Teething: There are two stages of normal teething. They usually occur between the ages of 4/6 months and again at 8/10 months. During teething chewing is essential for dogs. To soothe gums, apply a little baby gel.

Puppy Calming, Bonding & Grooming

All new experiences are stressful to our new puppy – sometimes we can help release the tension with calming exercises.

Shoulder, Chest & Leg/Foot Stress Release Method:
When calming is necessary, calmly, slowly and confidently stroke pup from side of neck downwards across left shoulder down to rump, then same down right side, then down chest area. Lift left ankle and hold warmly for the count of 5, gently shake foot. Repeat with right ankle. Continue until pup is calm.

AcuEar rub: Take the weight of say the left ear flap with the fingers of your left hand, and place your thumb on the top of the ear, slide the ear leather through your fingers and thumb, right to the tip of the ear. Do this several times, imagining your thumb is slowly winding up a watch, (embrace the entire ear as it slides through your fingers), so the position of the thumb could start in the middle of the ear, then the left side, then the right. The sliding action is important. Then do the right ear using your right hand. You could even do both ears at the same time! If the puppy is really stressed, at the end of each slide, press gently but firmly at the very tip of the ear. This is said to be an acupressure point for stress and shock.

Bonding & Grooming:

Bonding with pup is so important. There are many ways, but probably the best and most practical is to groom every day – quality time with puppy. Make sure the brush you use is kind (not one with spiky sharp teeth), but one that does the job effectively– plastic or rubber is good, (invest in a 'Zoom Groom'). Playtime is essential – a hearty game of tug, or fetch. Talk to your pup – communication's important – doesn't matter what you say – just talk. Also, a cuddle first thing in the morning, and last thing at night – works wonders. **Never yell at pup and NEVER ever hit him**

Digging Dog

Some think a dog digging is a sign of boredom, or destruction and this can obviously be part of it. However my personal opinion is that it's a natural part of canine behaviour and found more in dogs closest to the sociable wolf in breed, where either stress by solitary confinement or desire to build a natural den can be the cause. On recognising and accepting this, we would be adding to their stress should we scold our dog for digging, or concrete the entire area of our garden so it becomes impossible.

Compromise/Solution: Build a digging area for your dog – make sure this is adequate in size and should be no smaller in width or depth than the length of your dog (nose to end of tail). Construct the sides using wood. When re-filling the pit, use soil from areas where your dog has shown most interest before (if possible), and hide various goodies at various levels in the pit (pigs ears, safe artificial bones, and a few of your dog's favourite treats near the top). All objects should be concealed. You can allow your dog to see you construct his pit, but don't let him see you hide the goodies. Once built, restore all other areas dug by your dog to original state and cover the areas with garden chairs or put a sprinkler nearby. **Prepare for the game** – collect together a few pig's ears, fetch toys, and your sound tool (store them somewhere indoors, out of your dog's reach, but ready to grab immediately you next see your dog digging anywhere other than in his pit). Let your dog out into the prepared garden and peep through a window. After a few moments, call him in and praise him thoroughly – you're praising him for not digging, so make sure you do this in time. Let him out again and repeat this a few times (it's all part of the game and will take his mind off digging).

After doing this for a while, ignore your dog until s/he approaches an area where s/he cannot dig. Immediately, use **sound distraction** (one chink only, followed by prolonged verbal praise – **see 'Sound Distraction'**). Then, quickly run out to your dog (still praising) and throw one of the objects from your secret indoor store, into the pit — say 'dig' and start digging in the pit yourself for a few moments. Your dog should be so excited by this time that s/he'll probably play in the pit for ages. However, you may have to repeat this several times before s/he understands your change of attitude to digging and trust you enough to accept his pit. Until this happens, you will have to maintain supervised garden play.

Aggression

Why do some dogs show Aggression?

I must stress that the views expressed here are simply my opinions rather than cast iron facts. However those opinions are based on the observations and study carried out during thirty years experience in the field of dog training.

Studies on dog aggression are endless. Dominance aggression, fear aggression, genetic aggression, same-sex aggression, predatory aggression, jealousy, protective aggression, territorial aggression, rage syndrome, and so on. Perhaps we experts have made the subject sound a great deal more complicated than it really is.

My thoughts are as follows — aggression breeds aggression, and fear can turn to aggression. I would never say a dog is simply bad, or trying to be dominant. Usually, I believe aggression stems from fear, pain or inappropriate training, signals and responses from we humans: we have to remember that dogs mimic human behaviour and an aggressive response to a dog showing aggression (physical or verbal) will not resolve the problem. Physical punishment serves no long-term remedy but instead increases the chance of future attacks. A well respected person once wrote, 'The only form of aggressive measure that stops aggression is murder.' This, of course, is not intended to direct the reader to having the dog 'put to sleep' but to indicate that that no aggressive training will modify the dog's behaviour effectively, or long term.

The first step is assessment of the situation. With adopted dogs it's difficult as we cannot be sure of the dog's history. It's rare that a dog will show aggression without having suffered some form of abuse, frustration, pain, confusion, hormonal imbalance or illness. Therefore, if we are without historical records we should look at diet, health and possible pain first (** ask for veterinary guidance).

Ear infection or muck in ears **Paw injury** **Neck (disc) injury** — not always obvious and x-rays may be necessary (only ever use a flat collar or Halti). Many dogs suffer a painful existence (often undetected) due to inappropriate collars and/or heavy handed lead usage. Constant jerking and pulling can cause a whiplash effect, even with a flat collar.

Hormone imbalance** – Thyroid – (TSH-LowT4) / Progestogen

Fur balls – Groom your dog every day – Matted and tangled fur around the haunches for instance can cause a great deal of pain and has been known to result in temporary aggression, where carefully cutting these matts away has immediately solved the problem.

Diet – If you are feeding your dog a high protein complete meal, as well as red meat or tin food, you may well be feeding too high a level of protein which can create hyperactive behaviour. Try the following diet plan for 4 weeks and note daily any variances in behaviour.

- Rice (Boiled)
- Tripe, Chicken or White Fish (fresh or frozen)
- Recommended ** vitamin & mineral supplement
- One teaspoon sunflower or olive oil
- Occasional small amount of steamed potato peel & carrot peel (ensure they are not green or with eyes).

See your vet - Be sure your dog is not acting out of physical pain. For example, a rescue border collie was considered incurably aggressive. It transpired that the problem was that the dog hadn't been groomed for months, and the fur around his haunches was matted and tangled, causing him a lot of pain. As soon as the mats were cut away, he became docile and well-behaved. Another consideration is neck or disc injury caused by jerking on the lead – particularly if the dog has worn a chain check/choke collar. Loose lead training is absolutely essential in such cases. (see page 49)

Nutrition – Vitamins and minerals play an important part in your dog's emotional well-being, and can have a tremendous effect on their behaviour.

Don't yell – Many dogs stop misbehaving after their owners simply eliminate aggressive yelling. Shouting at our dog can actually stimulate aggression. Use distractions instead.

Always be positive – Although it's natural to feel nervous when your dog approaches another dog, and you may feel it's necessary to take a guarded warning tone, e.g. 'You'd better be good!' but what you're doing is stimulating the dog to feel aggressive. Try stimulating his social instincts: 'Is that your friend? Say hello! Good dog!'

Socialise – Provide a reasonable opportunity for your dog to interact with others in a positive way.

Play - Teach your puppy to 'fetch' or to play 'tug-of-war.' These games provide a safe, yet satisfying outlet for natural aggressive instincts.

Exercise Make certain your dog gets plenty of vigorous exercise - at least thirty minutes twice a day.

Ignore suggestions from trainers that include inflicting physical pain.

Once we've eliminated or addressed all the above, we can then move to other possible causes.

Aggression (TAPFA):

It is my belief that some aggressive behaviour stems from fear and nervousness, and is brought on by 'triggers'. Triggers can be odours, sounds, shapes, places, types of people, and types of clothing (e.g. hats, etc.) that the dog associates with previous situations where s/he has been conditioned to feel threatened. These triggers bring on the self-preservation instinct causing the dog to feel furtive and defensive and possibly develop phobias. The response to these phobias can be addressed immediately by 'sound interruption', followed by prolonged instant praise. In so doing we re-condition without adding additional triggers.

SoundPlay recognises there to be five stages known as TAPFA leading to aggressive moods. TAPFA can be explained as follows. Observing still frame video tapes has shown that all stages occur within just a split second, and always start with the 'Trigger' (as above), followed by 'Anticipation', followed by 'Pain' (physical or emotional), followed by 'Fear', and then 'Aggression'. Without re-conditioning we can do nothing about the 'Trigger'. However part of the re-conditioning is being aware and catching/distracting as near to the 'Anticipation' point as possible. This demands accurate timing. This is part of the reason sound distraction fails for those not adequately confident and/or aware. Negative physical and verbal correction may stop the behaviour momentarily - however, it does not teach nor does it address the root cause of the problem, serves no long term advantage in my opinion, and usually has the reverse effect.

Start as we mean to go on (with SoundPlay): We believe that if all puppies started lives the SoundPlay way, there wouldn't be any aggressive dogs. In-fact, we're so sure of SoundPlay, we believe this would also apply to wolves!

Address, don't repress: Unless a dog was severely abused by a former owner, or medically unfit, it should be fairly easy to cure his aggression. Indeed, almost all aggression problems in dogs are caused by human beings, lack of socialisation, bad training or bad example. Bear in mind that we can't cure aggression through dominance, punishment, or corrections. Such methods are only effective temporarily and can in fact teach the dog that aggression is the proper way to behave. We're always a little surprised when out with anything up to twenty dogs and a passer-by say, 'Isn't it wonderful to see them play so well together.' Dogs are very sociable animals and should usually get along together. See the fear and pain showing in poor Snowy's face and body language, as her owner pulls her on a tight lead ! Then see the difference after just 15 minutes SoundPlay loose-lead training. (page 49 – SoundPlay Classroom)

Snowy arrives on a Choke Collar.

These are still frames from a video film where the facial expressions couldn't be seen at normal video speed.

Now see the difference, after an hour!

Leads, Collars, Halti & Chinx:

Walking Lead: Our dog's lead should be flat leather or wide nylon – approx. 1 – 1.5 metre long.

Thick platted, Rope and chain leads are uncomfortable to the hands and should be avoided.

Long Teaching Lead: *Same style as walking lead, but as long as you can manage.*

Extending leads are OK for exercising our dog, but not ideal for teaching.

Collar: A **flat collar** that will extend over at least two cervical vertebrae; in a German Shepherd for instance, this might be 1" in width. The collar should fit snugly and always be sure there's extra length remaining for puppy/dog's growth. It's very important, while pup's still growing, that we check for comfort regularly - once a week is good. We have found it best NEVER to use chain, plaited, rope, prong or electric shock collars. We are particularly concerned that, even nowadays, some trainers are still advising dog owners to use the choke collar, when veterinary surgeons have been reporting the following injuries and damage to dogs from their use for over 20 years:

◆ Neuromuscular disorders resulting from constriction of the cervical region of the spine

◆ Rupture of the trachea

◆ Bruising to the ear and ear capsule, causing undue touch sensitivity in this region

◆ Epileptic fits, triggered by constriction of the blood supply to the brain.

Rescue Dogs: If we rescue a dog that we suspect has been trained harshly, using a chain check collar, we have the vet inspect for neck damage straight away. We then have to work at eliminating all memories the dog may have of previous pain & discomfort.

Halti: We approve of the Halti. It's important however that we purchase the correct size for our dog.

Harness: Some harnesses are badly designed and can cause pain and damage to the dog.

SoundPlay Chinx: For many teaching exercises we use sound distraction. An ordinary set of car keys can be used. SoundPlay chinx, all Kong products , Zoom Grooms and the Halti can be purchased from SoundPlay Dogs: accessories@soundplaydogs.com

Holding & Handling the Lead

Which side does our dog walk and which hand holds the lead?

We hold the lead with our right hand, but our dog walks on our left. Our left hand doesn't hold the lead, but is kept free to manoeuvre the slack (pass to right hand, up and down the lead), physically encourage and physically praise. Proper handling of the lead is important and it's best, as with most exercises, to first practice without our dog.

I always relate proper handling of the lead to when I first learned to drive – everything felt awkward at first. Then suddenly, it all clicked. Crunching the gears a few times was bad enough, but getting it wrong where my dog's neck was at stake would have been far more serious!!! Eric always said, training a dog is like ballroom dancing – we need to practice our footwork, timing, positioning, and co-ordination. So, here's a few exercises to practice, without dog please.

Also see 'Leads, Collars and Training Tools' and 'First time on the Lead' (page 22 & 42).

Lead manoeuvring exercise:

Ask a helper to stand next to you on your left, holding the clip-on end of the lead. Place lead loop around right wrist. (without twisting around wrist). Hold both hands out in-front, knuckles upwards and hold lead overhand with both hands. Practice taking in and letting out the slack (a bit like we're supposed to turn the steering wheel of our car). Right hand always returns to left hip, with left hand off lead. (see above). Repeat this a few times without your dog until you are sure you're holding and handling the lead properly.

IMPORTANT: Practice arm movements <u>before</u> you work with your dog.

Arm Movement Exercise:

Sit or stand with left arm behind back.

Swing right hand across your body with clenched fist and poke your left side (at waist level) with your thumb (your elbow should be relaxed and facing forward and knuckles should be facing upwards).

Twist wrist and turn thumb to face upwards –
keep hand clenched and at left side.

From that position and stance, move arm (just from the elbow) upwards and downwards so that your thumb swings up towards shoulder and back again (still pointing upwards).

There you have the angle and direction for directing to straight sit.

Left hand is free to direct dog inwards and towards, as you bend your knees to sit your dog. Feet remain still. (Keep shoulders back – don't bend forward)

SoundPlay Classroom

SoundPlay Classroom is designed to guide you through a 6-week training program. Each lesson will suggest reading material and exercises to be practised daily for 7 days – it's important that you stick to the program and practice every day. Although you may have read some of the course material already, we strongly suggest you refresh your memory by reading again, as and when suggested throughout the course. The program is suitable for puppies and dogs of any age. Please be diligent, consistent, enthusiastic, determined, and confident, but most of all Enjoy! You may email or write to me (c/o distributors) should you have difficulty – I shall endeavour to reply at absolute soonest. On occasion there may be a small administration charge – we will advise in advance should this be the case. Please see email addresses on back cover.

FIRST LESSON

Interruption of behaviour with sound distraction and praise: As from now, I suggest you adopt this method of correction, rather than any form of physical and/or verbal (not even a damaging glare). Of course, that's easier said than done – believe me, I know it takes some doing! Difficult enough for you, the reader to adapt to this new idea, but convincing other family members and friends that this is the route you choose to take, is far from easy. I'd been using 'sound distraction' and 'no physical correction' approach for many years, but when I first introduced to my own dogs, ('SoundPlay' methodology in total - no verbal corrections either) there was a certain amount of scepticism and doubt from even the closest of my family members. It was a totally new concept and people couldn't see how it could work – surely we can't control a dog without letting him know who's the boss?

My confidence and determination came from over a year's experimentation and observation while developing and perfecting the method, using several selections of behaviour problem dogs. The results were amazing.

Of course we need them to know who's in charge, but we don't need to bully, force, intimidate or confront – we need to be firm, fair, and consistent, but most of all we need to communicate in a way that dogs understand and respect. I think the easiest way to put the whole idea into perspective is to always remember that we can be verbally firm whenever we're instructing a dog 'what he should do' (once he's learned how to do it). However, we never engage in trying to instruct a dog 'what he must not do'. Therefore, we distract them from the behaviour we don't want, then immediately create a situation where they employ an alternative behaviour we do want, which we immediately reward with praise. The new behaviour then becomes far more worthwhile to our dog. Once 'conditioned' we can nearly always use 'come' as a default when interrupting a behaviour – therefore once learned (and as 'come' is a doing word), we can be as firm with the instruction as is necessary at that particular time.

Now to Heel

Before rushing into the 'heel', it's essential to explain that with SoundPlay, nothing is really taught independently. We have seen by observing and studying a significant number of video stills that sound will interrupt thought processes and behaviour, but the response is sometimes too minuscule for us to detect at normal speed. This is why we must praise immediately after the point of sound interruption.

We are praising for that unseen response. Therefore, first we have to condition our dog to respond to sound. (See 'Sound Distraction', page 14). Once the dog has learned to associate this sound as a sign to pay attention, or come to us, we can then teach the dog anything we feel appropriate.

The sound alone is worthless unless we condition our dogs to respond to it. To teach heel, we need to appreciate the importance of timing, co-ordination, body language, correct use of praise, and we also have to learn how to hold and handle the lead (please read again: Holding & Handling the lead). So, accepting that the dog has already learned to understand the 'sound interruption' means 'Hey you – attention please' - then we can proceed with teaching other things.

First HEEL

One of the biggest mistakes we make with heel is allowing the lead to become tight before saying heel. This is teaching our dog that the 'heel' sound means tight lead and sore neck. Also, yelling heel once our dog's already pulling isn't teaching 'where heel is'. It will create an aversion to the sound of the word heel and reverse the assumed teaching process. Therefore, before we can expect our dog to know where heel is, we have to show him.

We do this while in a stationery position (sit/heel). Then teach our dog to move with, and at the same speed as, our left leg. We have to consider the rhythm of our walking and the length of our legs compared to our dogs. Shorter, quicker paces are usually required. Also read First time on the lead, page 22.

Lesson One:
Dog sitting beside left leg. Lead in right hand – left hand off lead (see holding and handling lead, page 43). Say 'Heel', and instantly praise. End of exercise – play with dog.

You may feel praising the dog for apparently doing nothing is inappropriate – however, hearing 'heel' at the same point as the sound is linked to a pleasant association with the sound of the word 'heel'.

Repeat the above 3 times.

Now we can move on to teaching our dog that 'heel' can also mean 'move with our left leg'.

Lesson Two:
Repeat lesson one, but as you say 'Heel' take one step to your right - **immediately praise** (for at least 10 seconds) - doesn't matter if dog moves – it's important to praise immediately after you say 'heel.'

End of exercise - play with dog.

Lesson Three: Repeat Lesson One

Lesson Four: Repeat Lesson Two, but take two paces to your right.
Lesson Five: Repeat Lesson One
Lesson Six: Repeat Lesson Two, but take one pace forward – LEFT foot first.
Lesson Seven: Repeat Lesson Six, but take two paces forward – LEFT foot first.
Lesson Eight: Repeat Lesson One.

From here on, you can begin to increase paces forward, but if dog at any time fails to pay attention, about turn, (keep feet moving) and trot in opposite direction as you say 'heel' and immediately praise enthusiastically. Never say two 'heels' together without praise separating them. **Lead must never become tight and we never yell at our dog.**
The above can be achieved in half an hour. The aim is to have our dog wanting to walk with us, without force, fear and pain.

Does my dog have to 'heel' all the time when on a lead?

Seeing a dog beautifully walking to heel is a sight to be seen, but sometimes it really isn't necessary in my opinion. Struggling to have our dog 'heeling' continually on the lead can take all the enjoyment out of quality time with our dog. Social walks can be relaxed but we don't want our dog pulling. Pulling on the lead where the collar becomes tight will cause a resistance where the dog will pull harder – we have to keep the lead and collar loose! This is why, along with heel, I also teach my dogs 'loose'. Loose simply means 'no tight lead'. Once our dog understands the 'loose' word, we can instruct accordingly while casually walking our dog. I've designed many exercises for this purpose - here's two.

Stop, Look & Learn Exercise

I make it a rule to do this exercise every time I first put my dog on lead, and also at anytime it's not convenient to address tight lead in any other way. The exercise is designed to enhance attraction to the handler and lead training generally. It's very simple, but accuracy and consistency is essential!
All walking members of the family should be able to exercise 'Stop, Look & Learn'. The exercise begins while you're still in the house – en route to the door is good. It could take you several minutes to reach the door, so give yourself plenty of time. Teaching takes time and patience – we want the

dog to learn, not be forced. Please use 'stop, look & learn' at every opportunity - the results are amazing!

1. Attach Lead to Flat Collar or Halti. Hold lead in right hand – with dog at our front, say 'Come on' and immediately praise – (continue to praise as dog approaches). Guide dog in to your left and then round anti-clockwise to sit straight at heel by left leg.

   Direct dog in and around in a small <u>anti-clockwise</u> 'about turn' by our left side. Say 'Heel, Straight Sit, Stay.' Don't praise. Time saying sit, during the last 90 degrees, so dog doesn't overshoot the position. Use left hand if necessary to position dog in a straight sit to heel.

2. Move forward say Heel and praise (left leg first). Say Heel and praise each time left foot hits the ground. If/when dog moves forward away from heel, STOP – DO and SAY NOTHING. Just stop, say nothing at all – don't move, and wait for however long it takes for dog to <u>look</u> back at you: then <u>immediately</u> PRAISE PRAISE PRAISE (<u>NO other commands</u> and don't re-position dog back to heel). We're teaching the dog to be aware, and also to realise that pulling isn't getting him anywhere! The act of looking back (turning back) is rewarded with praise. Our dog learns to always keep us in his sights, always pay attention, and that a tight lead is of no advantage!

3. Walk on and repeat for as long as you like. Doing this consistently and accurately will eventually result in your dog looking back at you every time he approaches the end of the lead and/or when you stop walking. After a while, he will actually slacken the lead as tension begins - when this happens, say 'loose' and praise. It's a very simple and basic measure to improve leisure walking when heel training is not always possible. Please don't become frustrated and give up on this exercise – some dogs take longer to learn than others – also, some enjoy testing us out! A dog that's perhaps been used to harsh jerking and pulling will take longer to trust that this is all about to stop. Once we've earned our dog's trust, everything improves – far more than we could ever imagine.

Loose Lead, Recall & Sound Conditioning Exercise

Training Tools required: Long training lead, <u>flat collar</u> and SoundPlay Chinx or set of keys.

(Most pet stores will stock long training leads, or we can supply you – average price today is £8.00)

Dog on long lead, safe quiet outside environment (not garden) – dog roaming freely. Immediately and EVERY time dog almost reaches end of lead, say

'LOOSE' then praise. If your dog hits the end, and lead's already tight, loosen the slack a little as you say 'loose' — then praise (keep a little lead back to enable loosening). Then say 'Come', PRAISE PRAISE PRAISE as you turn and trot away from dog (maintain fast foot movement as you turn).

Every third or forth time dog approaches end of lead (before taut), say 'Come' with chink, TROT opposite direction IMMEDIATELY, while PRAISING (on the spot if necessary). We want our dog to believe there's something amazing and important ahead of us — we BOTH need to go seek. We're working together as a team. Lead must be slack. The essential and excited tone while praising is what will bring our dog flying towards us.

As dog arrives near enough (this can take some manoeuvring — we may need to turn again a few times repeating as above, to draw dog closer and closer), touch ONCE on dog's shoulder or back and say 'OFF YOU GO' as we fling our hands in a waving off motion. We don't want our dog to think coming back to us always means home time, restriction, or prison. We want him to see it as a vital part of our work, going off, coming back in.

Never walk towards dog: we're the guide and we lead the way. On occasions, we can interact a little more before sending off again (a game of catch my hands, or watch the hands clap, or pat the ground), then send off again, then back to work. Remember always to say 'LOOSE' at times you're not saying 'COME'.

Please note: It's important that we praise immediately as we say 'Loose' or 'Come', and with 'Come' continue to praise continually until dog arrives near enough to touch and send off again. Use every bit of energy to encourage in. If everyone in the park doesn't think we're crazy, you're probably not putting enough into it.

LESSON TWO

What are we teaching?

Body Language and Verbal Communication: When teaching a dog we must always use consistent, co-ordinated and precise body signals along with every verbal instruction taught. I always advise my students to imagine their dog can be either deaf or blind at anytime, and to never rely solely on our voice, nor our body. The two have to work together when teaching so that if either were eliminated, the other would be as reliable on its own.

Canine Body Language: In nature, the wolf does not adorn itself with a collar, so we must presume that the body postures and sensitivities of the dog have evolved without collars in mind. Wolves and dogs communicate by the position and hair cover on the body and tail, by facial expressions and chemical signals. They are not particularly vocal; thus their response to complex voice commands from human beings does not come easily or naturally. One can conclude therefore, that the traditions of spoken commands and tugs at the neck of a dog, does not exploit the natural response tendencies of the species. *Dr. Roger Mugford – 1980*

Walking on the lead / Heel: The word heel means nothing to our dog until we teach him. We have to show our dog where 'heel' is... not where it isn't !!! For instance, if we have our dog walk beside us and yell 'heel' once he's gone forward on a tight lead, we're actually teaching him 'heel' is in front of us, pulling on the lead – he will associate the word 'heel' with a sore neck. The Opposite Nose Exercise is an excellent way to teach a dog how rewarding it is to walk beside us, and how wonderful the word 'heel' really is! It's not a very easy exercise, but I have to say it's one I'm particularly proud of.

Loose: Sometimes it's great to walk with our dogs leisurely. We don't necessarily need them to 'heel', but we do like them to have a loose lead. Our dog should never have to endure the discomfort of a tight collar. Bad heel training can actually cause pulling, injury to our dog – and other behaviour problems, such as aggression.

Coming Back: This is one of the first exercises we address at SoundPlay classes. Many of our conditioning exercises are introduced while teaching recall.

Sit: We can make use of sit to teach 'stationary heel position'. Generally, most dogs will sit happily once we stop walking. Some owners like to have their dog sit prior to feeding – a gesture of obedience and appreciation that is then rewarded.

Stand: Personally, I think this is as important, if not more so, than sit (also see page 26).

Stay: Teaching 'stay' is easy as long as we employ accurate body language while teaching 'heel.'

For instance, always move off with our left foot first when heeling, and with our right foot first when staying.

Down: There's nothing submissive in the way we teach 'down' – a dog can be successfully be taught this without any force in just a few moments.

Pack Exercise: Every Sunday afternoon, we invite anyone from our home-town to join us socialising our dogs. Once everyone's arrived, the first thing we do is 'set the boundaries' and 'organise the pack', off lead. Sometimes, a couple of newcomer dogs are on long-leads at first, but not for long. Dogs are the best teachers of dogs. Any pushy newcomer is quickly shown the ropes by our well-behaved regular canines! We don't have fights – it's a sight to be seen; a minimum of 17 dogs running, playing and communicating as a pack and remaining absolutely within the boundaries we pack leaders have set them. The area we meet is a popular dog walking park – many other dogs visit, and walk through the park while we're there – visiting dogs tend not to move into our pack territory and our pack of dogs ignore them totally and remain within the boundaries set. The pack exercise is the first event of the afternoon – try it:

PACK EXERCISE

Please have a family meeting before this exercise, ensuring every family member fully understands what to do. This exercise can be done either on or off a long lead. Dogs that cannot be trusted should not be allowed off-lead. The 'pack' exercise is great for the building of your status relationship with your dog. It requires about an hour to perform.

You are going to be walking with all of the immediate members of your family, and your dog, in a large square. You'll need an area large enough to walk a 100ft. square, including additional space to provide clearance for the length of your long lead. Find an area at least 140-ft. square. Gather in a close knit group, and proceed to walk as one unit from your starting point - about one step per second. Don't look at your dog, or at least try not to let your dog see you look at him. Everyone must remain **silent** unless he looks at you, moves along with you, or moves in towards you.

Every time he does so, **everyone (together)** praises him. Anytime he doesn't follow the group, totally ignore him. At each corner of the 100ft Square stop (everyone) and remain absolutely silent for a 30 seconds. Then continue to praise as and when applicable (see above) and continue walking to next corner. Continue walking this square for approx. 20 minutes. You should notice your dog coming to you more and more frequently and actually stopping with you at the corners (perhaps laying down to rest). After walking the area as above for 20 minutes you can relax and play with your dog, but don't take the play outside the walked boundary. Next time you do the exercise, invite friends who have dogs, but remember not to talk while walking the course. Try doing this exercise every day for a week and then once a week thereafter.

CATCH ME EXERCISE

'CATCH ME' is a fun way of improving heel and recall – It's what we call a

'conditioning' exercise – The exercise does not demand a 'perfect heel' - our aim is to excite and motivate our dog. We manipulating our dog's positioning, with dog reaching highest satisfaction while 'at heel' and when 'coming to us' (catching up with us). This exercise demands high levels of mental and physical energy – if we're not feeling exhausted after ten minutes, we're doing it wrongly.

'Catch Me' is an 'off-lead' exercise.
You'll need a ball or Cool Kong on a rope.
Bounce ball or Cool Kong while running/teasing in zigzag motion in front of dog – encourage dog to jump high at ball. **At point** of extreme excitement, (while paws are in air, if possible), turn swiftly so that you put dog at heel position, <u>as you say 'heel' (once only)</u> and **_immediately_** praise, praise,

praise. Run off again, slapping left leg with left hand (holding ball in your right), - keep praising for at least 15 seconds, (praise must be non-physical). Repeat several times – increasing level of excitement each time you run off - try to lose your dog, while still praising – s/he has to catch you, but don't make it easy. As s/he approaches, slap left leg, bounce ball (catch it), and turn right or about turn. As you turn right or about turn, - say 'come on then', followed by immediate praise, praise, praise, while running off in opposite direction – keep praising and slapping that left leg. 'Heel' is then said every time you find your dog at heel. Phew – fall to the floor and wrestle for a while – repeat exercise one last time, then have a cup of coffee. Repeat **every day** for a week.

Please note: Once you become efficient with your timing, you can also use the 'sound tool' (one chink only) each time you run off and say 'come-on then'.

LESSON THREE

Opposite Nose Heel Exercise

Make it a rule to do this as a warming up exercise. Opposite Nose Heel Exercise is not easy – however, once you get the knack, the results are truly amazing! Accuracy and consistency is essential!

1. Attach Lead to Collar. Hold lead in right hand. Tell dog it's Work Time!!! 'Hey we're gonna do some WORK!!!' With dog facing at our front, say 'Come' and praise. Hold lead correctly in right hand, using left hand if

necessary to position dog in a straight sit to heel position. (Guide in from your front, to your left – on reaching left leg about-turn **dog** anti-clockwise round to heel) – say 'Heel, Straight Sit, Stay.' Don't praise.

2. Move forward (left foot first) as you say 'Heel', with immediate praise. Continue to say 'Heel', with immediate praise each time left foot hits the ground. Immediately dog moves away from heel (even a couple of inches), redirect yourself to face the exact opposite direction to that which your dog's nose is pointing – **keep feet moving** (fast small paces). Each time you change direction, say 'come on' and praise, praise, praise while moving off in that Opposite Nose Direction. Enough enthusiasm and our dog will chase after us. Important: as soon as dog reaches heel again, say 'Heel' and immediately praise. DON'T STOP MOVING YOUR FEET – DON'T TUG ON THE LEAD (walk on the spot if necessary, but keep facing/moving in opposite direction). We can imagine we're working from the centre of a clock. Dog's nose points to 5, we walk away to 11, dog's nose points 3, we walk to 9, and so on. We have to watch, concentrate, maintain constant motion, verbal communication and always remain alert – it's hard work and we soon become dizzy!!!

3. After 5 minutes or so the exercise is over. Play fetch for a few moments. Remember: **We NEVER say heel when our dog IS NOT AT HEEL**

Recall & Heel Sound Conditioning

Please note: We are teaching the dog that returning to us is enjoyable – 'come' doesn't mean prison, or time to go home, or 'stop enjoying yourself'.

We want our dog to come back to us because s/he wants to. Saying 'Heel' (just once) as dog arrives at heel will help confirm where 'heel' is. We don't need to continue heeling – we're merely confirming the position.

Dog on long lead – allow dog to roam within area to end of lead (be casual). Walk away from dog at all times – LOOSE LEAD (practice manoeuvring the lead – letting out, drawing in – never tight).

Casual walk - as dog approaches end of lead (before taut), ***say 'Come' and chink once (same time) – *immediate'* praise praise praise, while running in opposite direction. Maintain praise until dog arrives along side – say 'heel'(once) and praise – continue praising while slowing pace to a walk. If dog moves off again from heel, about turn, (small fast trotting paces) and repeat from ***.

Please note:

◆ DON'T wait for dog to respond to the word COME before praising… the praise MUST be IMMEDIATE PROLONGED and EXCITED.

◆ While running away, we may have to trot on the spot, (quicker the better) or zig zag in order to keep the lead loose. We must maintain praise until dog reaches us.

◆ We take care not to walk in towards our dog.

Repeat over and over, until our dog watches for any change of direction, and starts coming in automatically. Repeat exercise at least 15 minutes, every day for a week.

Sit/Stay (Stage One)

We start teaching 'sit/stay' while teaching 'heel'. The dog is taught that heel means 'remain with the left leg' - if the left leg moves, the dog has to move, if the leg is still, or only the right leg moves, the dog has to be still. If we move the right leg without saying 'heel', the dog should remain still, because nothing has been requested. **Hence a stay.**

We **teach/confirm** this by labelling the 'doing nothing' with the word 'stay', **plus** suitable body language (we never under-estimate body language). We don't praise our dog, nor do we use the dog's name while in 'stay' - we give a physical signal for 'stay' using our right hand held outright, with fingers pointed to the sky - and we ALWAYS release from the stay with a specific and consistent, well timed instruction.

Sit/Stay (although important) is just an introduction to 'stay' and cannot be considered as reliable as 'down/stay'. Once our dog is 'straight sitting' beside us at heel (paying attention with eye contact), say 'STAY', and carefully move right foot only, one pace to the right (don't move left foot). **Don't use dog's name and don't praise dog until the 'release' at end of exercise.** Our dog must not move (not even an inch) – if s/he does, or even nudges towards us, we immediately re-position to exact spot originally left, with dog facing same start direction. *We don't use dog's name, nor do we praise while repositioning – just 'sit, stay'.*

◆ If our dog lies down, we quickly go to the front of dog, shuffle feet onto our dogs front paws and say 'Sit', then 'Stay.' No need to use dog's name, and still no praise (praise comes only at release).

◆ If our dog stands up, we immediately say 'SIT', then 'stay', while repositioning our dog in exact position, facing exactly the same direction as when we began. No need to use dog's name, and still no praise (praise comes only at release).

◆ Once our dog has stayed for, say, 10 seconds without nudging towards us, laying down, or standing up, we can return our right foot and release our dog by physically and verbally praising.

◆ Once we've sat our dog at heel and said 'stay', we don't use the word heel at any future point during this exercise.

Release: The release is an essential part of teaching stay – it must be an exact and consistent' physical and verbal action that gives our dog permission to move. We should all develop our own individual signal for the release from stay. It can go something like this: **Verbal action: 'HEY**, there's a good boy, ... praise praise praise". **Physical action:** One pace forward with left foot first – bend knees and give physical praise reward. (I try to get

Whisky to jump up and give me a kiss, while tapping my shoulders and squealing 'up' 'up' 'up' - or the like. Some people with Border Collies can actually get their dog to jump right up on their shoulders. Important: No matter how many times our dog moves, we must continue to reposition him (as above), until he has remained still for at least 10 seconds, and we're ready to complete the stay. This can be a lengthy exercise, should our dog insist on moving every time we move away. However, at this stage, it's better to 'stay' our dog for 10 seconds successfully, than to attempt longer and fail.

Next: Exactly as stage one, but we take one full pace to the right (both feet) – otherwise exactly the same. That's it for now – do NO MORE THAN THIS, but be exact in what you do.

Staying with my dog

Imagine an invisible beam running from our dogs eyes straight to our own eyes —if the beam is broken even for an instant, mend the beam by moving our right hand swiftly towards the break, which is always just in front of our dog's eyes. Once repaired, slowly back off to our original position. We slowly circle the dog, as if on a tightrope. As we pass a certain point behind the dog, we watch his eyes follow until he can't quite see our face and spins his head round frantically (so as not to break that beam).

There are no words to describe this feeling – it's stronger than 'mood', 'concentration', 'obedience', 'control', – it's more like 'focus', way out, hypnotic, two souls connected, magical: the feeling when teaching 'stay' is that nothing else exists – just me and my dog, here in this place that can't be touched by anything or anyone. That invisible beam is life or death - it cannot and will not be broken - imagine our dog on one remaining chunk of ice in the middle of the ocean:– if he moves a fraction he'll fall and drown. We use every ounce of energy in our body and mind to maintain that unique connection. The excitement's there, being stored – waiting to explode, static but ever showing in those wondrous eyes. Then, when the times right, the 'release' and an explosion of excitement! **This** is the moment the dog learns (the more excited, the more reliable next time).

LESSON FOUR

Daily Exercise Practice:

Sit/Stay (Stage Two)

Follow the instructions exactly as Sit/Stay (Stage One), but then continue by taking one pace forward (right foot first), turn and face dog. The exact same rules apply should our dog move. We should only leave our dog staying for 30 seconds on the first occasion, then up the time by say 30 seconds each session. We achieve far more by satisfactorily completing a 30 second stay, than pushing it and failing on an attempt at 60 seconds. Once we've achieved a minute stay from one pace to the front, we can increase the distance a little. The exercise is not completed until we can return to our dog, wait a few seconds and 'release'. The Sit/Stay exercise can be done on, or off lead. (Don't forget hand signal)

Sit, Wait & Recall Exercise

We teach 'wait' as a temporary form of 'stay'. Body language, voice tone and our reaction should our dog move is exactly the same – all that changes is the word. We use 'stay' when we are not intending to call our dog to us, or when we are not intending to alter our dog's position. However, the 'wait' is used mostly for testing – as in recall and position change. For instance, we can leave our dog in a 'sit/wait', and then call our dog to us. Another time, we can leave our dog in a 'sit/wait', and reposition to 'down.' Reposition exercises are a little advanced at this stage, but the recall from 'sit/wait' should be achievable once we've adequately practised everything up to lesson 4. Before attempting 'sit, wait & recall' we must have secured a reliable 'sit/stay' (for say 2 minutes, off lead).

We start by sitting our dog at heel. We say 'Wait' and move off with right foot. We can begin with a distance of say 5 ft away – turn and face dog, keep right hand in position, indicating 'wait' until we're ready to call our dog. Pause for a count of say 30 seconds before throwing arms out to sides and saying 'Come', then praise for the entire duration our dog comes in. That's it. Some people like to finish with a sit to front, or a sit at heel. Should our dog move before being called, we must reposition and start again.

LESSON FIVE

Daily Exercise Practice:

Time to 'Proper Heel'

By this time, assuming we've practised all the sound conditioning and pack exercises, we should have no problem interrupting behaviours or calling our dog to us while on long lead, and for most of us, off lead by now. Now we come to a more difficult task – 'proper heel' on lead. Here is the start routine every time we need to 'proper heel' our dog:

Start routine: With dog on lead, relax and praise. Take a deep breath, face dog and say 'Hey, we're going to WORK.' Take a few paces backwards, say 'come'; immediately praise and continue praising as dog approaches. Guide dog in and towards our left side, and about turn, anti-clockwise round to the heel position. Say 'heel straight sit/stay.' No praise (remember 'stay' and 'wait' are words where we don't praise immediately after). We don't want to confuse the dog by delaying here, – this isn't a 'stay' exercise. We make sure we're holding the lead correctly and standing upright (shoulders back). Walk forward **(left foot first)** saying 'heel' (dog's name first if you like). **Immediately praise and continue praising all the time dog remains at heel.**

What to do when dog leaves heel position

If dog refuses to walk, before lead becomes taut, return to dog and start off again – this time more encouragement and happier 'heel' - smaller bouncier paces, click left hand fingers or anything else that you feel will make pup feel more at ease. (Sometimes tight leads, tugging and jerking on the lead leaves a dog reluctant to walk at all – should we feel this could be signifi-cant, we have to build trust again). Praise immediately after every 'heel' instruction. If we can't get pup to move, we can try turning to face him, say 'come', praise praise praise, while taking tiny paces backwards. As pup moves towards us, quickly turn, continue walking and say 'heel' as pup reaches the spot – finish there with loads of praise – then start again.

If dog walks on forward - <u>immediately</u> dog passes the heel point, about turn, taking small bouncy paces and walk off in the opposite direction. Say 'come-on, come-on, come-on' (**NOT** heel), then praise praise praise. When dog catches up, and exactly at the point s/he's at heel, say 'heel' praise praise praise (**never** say 'heel' when dog is out of position).

If dog walks too far to the left of us - <u>immediately</u> and long before the lead becomes taught, turn right, taking small bouncy paces and walk off to the right .... say 'come-on, come-on, come-on' (**NOT** heel) praise praise praise. When dog catches up, and exactly at point s/he's at heel..... say 'heel' praise praise praise. **Never** say 'heel' when dog is out of position.

Testing

Once we've practised the above daily for a few days, there are many ways to test the 'heel'. Work with someone else who's training if possible – here are just a few suggestions:

Set up a course: A line of rocks about 5 ft apart (anything will do, it's just a visual marker). Heel dog through the course, weaving in and out the rocks. This will make us think about direction and concentrate more on what we're trying to achieve. Having someone else take a turn will give us incentive to work more efficiently – it'll also make it fun! We have a wonderful time with our groups – a happy disposition works wonders while training dogs. We can even set up a couple of small hurdles and have our dog sit and wait, then jump the hurdle on route to us, on recall.

LESSON SIX

Daily Exercise Practice:
All exercises from all previous lessons
Fun Down

Fun Down

Stage One:
Play 'tug' and 'bouncy ball' with 'kong on a rope' (or rope toy) while squatting or kneeling in front of dog – use voice to encourage eye contact and walk backwards slowly.

Continue until dog is excited. Then crawl backwards while bouncing and rolling kong/ball lower and lower, and teasingly encourage chase-play.

When dog's at peak of excitement, let go of toy, hold dogs front legs/ankles (carefully) one in each hand (our aim is, to do this without dog realising). QUICKLY, gently and firmly (we must not splay legs or hurt dog), bring dog's legs toward us and say **'DOWN'** (excited tone) then immediately, praise praise praise. Lower our head onto top of dog's neck to further encourage a relaxed 'down' (all this is done in a split second).

We mustn't frighten dog and s/he doesn't have to stay down - continue praise whatever the result

(at this stage, we're teaching the word/sound 'DOWN').

Exercise over.

I cannot stress enough how important it is that our dog doesn't feel intimidated by this exercise. It must be seen as part of the game – the dog arrives down without knowing quite how he got there !

Then, loads of praise for what seemed so simple. Also, it was oh so exciting getting there.

Repeat 3 times – then play with dog for 5 minutes.

Repeat every day for a week – do nothing to create fear or anxiety.

We do not agree with the 'submission theory' where the dog sees going down as submitting.

The down can be a lifesaver – It has to be respected, not feared.

Next comes Down Stay – Once a dog has been properly taught to down/stay, 10 minutes out of sight would not be considered at all difficult. SoundPlay Classroom 2 shows how this can be achieved, plus many other essentials - SoundPlay Classroom 2 is included in 'More Essentials for the Domestic Dog Training'

AN ARTICLE BY AUTHOR UNKNOWN

Someone sent me the following article, written by an unknown author. I've included it exactly as sent because there's some interesting reading. To edit it doesn't seem right somehow – perhaps the unknown author will recognise his or her work and allow me to give credit, when publishing my next book....

Puppy Socialization

Starting one week after you get your puppy (age 8 or 9 weeks), get him out one day a week to a new situation he has never seen before. This takes some planning, but is worth the effort.

8 Weeks: A walk (off leash) in a meadow or pasture with medium tall grass. Keep him with you by voice. Encourage him to climb over a little mound of dirt or a log. *Praise* his efforts to do something he has never done before. Walk just fast enough that he has to strain very slightly to keep up with you. At this age his desire to stay with you is very keen. Capitalize on that. The walk should take no more than 20 minutes.

9 Weeks: Another walk, this time in the woods. He is in taller grass and weeds. He must occasionally climb over small logs (just big enough to be a challenge). He goes up the hill, down the hill, over the rocks, maybe down a small bank. The perfect setup is where he goes across a small creek. He gets wet up to the chest. He scrambles up the bank to follow you. He goes through a thick carpet of leaves that crunch when he walks. Encourage him all the way. Praise him for meeting the challenge. The walk takes about 20 minutes.

10 Weeks: The same as age 9 weeks but a bit more difficult. Occasionally hide momentarily from him when he is distracted in the woods. Watch him. Does he notice you are missing? If he does, and starts to look for you, suddenly appear and praise profusely. If he doesn't look for you, toss a pebble to make him notice you are missing. Then call him from your hiding place. When he starts to look for you, appear and praise him. This will teach him, as it is repeated time and time again, to watch you when you are out in the woods, instead of you having to constantly be watching where he is. This makes him take that responsibility of staying with you. Play this game over and over through many weeks until you cannot hide from him because he is always watching. This only works when started young.

11 Weeks: Take him swimming. You hold him and wade out to knee deep water. Point him toward shore and gently let him go. Be sure he gets his head up and he heads for shore. Have someone on shore encouraging him in a positive way. Another way to approach this is to entice him into the water by going in yourself and encouraging him to follow. Do not throw him in! When you are through get him out and dry him off and go home. Don't let him get chilled.

12 Weeks: Take a trip to the farm. Let him see cows, horses, chickens and whatever else you can find. This time you can keep him on leash. Make sure he is safe from the animals and let him get close enough to sniff. This outing can take 20 or more minutes. You have a positive attitude about all this. Be nonchalant about it all, as if this is what every 12 week old pup does.

13 Weeks: Take him on leash to town. Walk him on a main street with medium to light foot traffic. He sees and hears cars, trucks and heavy street traffic. He passes by many people walking bicycles, delivery men with hand trucks, etc. This should be a short outing about 10 minutes. Praise him lavishly for positive behaviour. Be nonchalant and very encouraging. When you get back to the car, lay on the praise for his remarkable feats of courage.

14 Weeks: A trip to the beach or some other special place he has never been. Perhaps a trip to the local grade school front lawn when all the children are pouring out. Let the kids stop and pet him. Let him see and be in the crowd.

15 Weeks: Another trip to town.

16 Weeks: Your pup's major learning age of his entire life is now over. Hopefully you have given him a very wide range of experiences. If you have done all this faithfully you will have taught him the most important thing of all to learn and it will stay with him the rest of his life, enabling him to continue to learn throughout his lifetime.

17 to 21 Weeks: This is a bad time to subject your pup to stress, such as plane trips, a stay at the vets, boarding kennel or any threatening situation. Many pups act very fearful at this age. This should be a quiet time in their lives.

Unknown Author

Some more of the animals in my life